365 DAYS
OF ENCOURAGING
YOU TO
ATTACK
LIFE

MARC HAYFORD POWER BOOK SERIES
VOLUME II

Printed in the United States of America
First Printing, 2018

ISBN-13: 9781791541682

ACKNOWLEDGEMENTS

THANK YOU CHRISTINA,

KANE,

JAYDA

AND

HARRISON.

You inspire me to fight hard to inspire others.

THIS IS DEDICATED

to the one who needs to know that

today they do not walk alone.

INTRODUCTION

WHEN I RELEASED MY FIRST BOOK *Get Up (Encouraging You To Attack Life)* in the early part of 2018, it became a number one, best seller in Amazon's "Self Help" category within four hours of it's release. I was blown away.

What blew me away even more were the responses that I've received from people who have read it. Regardless of age, color, background, social status or location, I had people sharing with me how the positive reinforcement and mindset of the book helped them with whatever their trials and circumstances were. It was humbling.

What I've learned throughout the year from all the interaction with the travel, assemblies, seminars and speaking events is this: We all need to be poured into. Daily. And, we all need to be on purpose with fighting through fear, self doubt, false self limitations and constantly holding back.

The purpose of this book is to remind you daily that you have greatness inside of you. It is created to inspire, challenge, motivate and ultimately propel you to appreciate each day. This book will encourage you to take control of YOUR life, instead of allowing your life to be constantly controlled.

At the first of each month expect to see a "#Mindhack." This is meant to give a sobering slap so you can dive into the next thirty days with intention. I've also selected certain quotes from "Get Up," as well as other newly created ideas that you will benefit from throughout your month. This "Power Book" has the same mindset and direction of "Get Up," and it is meant to serve you daily.

Now, you've just been handed 365 days of daily inspiration to attack life. So, pick your head up, get your feet moving and let's get at it. GET UP!

ALWAYS

IN

YOUR

CORNER

- MARC HAYFORD

365 DAYS
OF ENCOURAGING
YOU TO ATTACK LIFE

ISAIAH 40:31

"BUT THEY THAT WAIT UPON THE *Lord*

SHALL RENEW THEIR STRENGTH;

THEY SHALL MOUNT UP

WITH WINGS AS *eagles*;

THEY SHALL *run*, AND NOT BE WEARY;

AND THEY SHALL WALK,

AND *not* FAINT."

JANUARY 1

#MINDHACK

THREE WEEKS FROM NOW ALL THE resolutions will have melted away. But, you don't have any "resolutions" because you have life goals. This is YOUR year. Don't sit back and hope for "it" to happen. MAKE "it" happen! GET UP!!

JANUARY 2

LET'S START THIS OFF RIGHT.

If it doesn't serve you, it needs to be released.

JANUARY 3

I SUCKED IN CHEMISTRY, BUT I became the president of my high school the first time they put me in front of a microphone with an audience. Today, I can't tell you about properties or substances, but I get paid to speak. Don't focus on what you're NOT good at. Go hard on what you ARE good at and work to become GREAT at it.

JANUARY 4

TGIF = THE GRIND INCLUDES FRIDAY.

JANUARY 5

ABRAHAM LINCOLN'S FIANCE DIED,
his businesses failed, he lost multiple
elections and yet somehow he still became
the 16th president. I think you can make
it past breakfast. Be strong today.

JANUARY 6

JUST TO BE CLEAR,

I believe in you.

JANUARY 7

BE DIFFERENT FROM THE OTHER 98% of the world. Focus on what you DO want, not what you DON'T want.

JANUARY 8

YOU CAN READ THESE AND BE
inspired with good vibes all you want.
If you don't get up and put in the work,
you just donated to me. I don't like being
your charity of choice. Let's go.

JANUARY 9

GOOD MORNING. WE'LL ACCEPT
screaming, crying, scratching, crawling and
anything in the "whatever it takes" category.
Currently, we are not accepting quitting as
a means of resolution. Thank you for your
understanding. We appreciate your patience
at this time. Now go do what it takes.

JANUARY 10

YOU'LL SEE IT WHEN YOU BELIEVE it.

JANUARY 11

VISIONARIES ALWAYS SEEM CRAZY

to people that have no vision.

JANUARY 12

IF YOU ARE COMFORTABLE,
you're in trouble. Get uncomfortable asap.

JANUARY 13

YOU CAN MAKE A DIFFERENCE OR
you can make an excuse. See? You have options.

JANUARY 14

STOP FOCUSING ON LOOKING GOOD
and start focusing on GETTING good. Lose
the filter and fall in love with the grind.

JANUARY 15

STOP TRYING TO FIT IN WITH THE
crowd. You should be scared to death
of being just like everyone else.

JANUARY 16

YOU HAVE TWO OPTIONS IN LIFE.
You can be the hammer, or you can be the
nail. Be the freakin' HAMMER. Start swinging!

JANUARY 17

TIMOTHY 1:7 READS "FOR GOD HATH not given us the spirit of fear; but of power, and of love, and of a sound mind." So that anxiety is false. You are more powerful than you know. Today share love and be aware.

JANUARY 18

I WANT YOU TO READ THIS OUT loud. *"*I am in control. I am the boss. I have all the power that I need inside of me to unlock great things and change circumstances for the better. The change starts and thrives with me."

JANUARY 19

STOP HOLDING BACK. YOU'LL NEVER
be this young again. Do it today.

JANUARY 20

TO CHANGE YOUR LIFE, YOU NEED
to change your life. Start thinking
and acting different.

JANUARY 21

IT'S HARD FOR THEM TO IGNORE
you when you refuse to quit.

JANUARY 22

I COACH FOOTBALL. I EXPRESS urgency, discipline and a mindset of outworking everyone else. We win. Just sayin'.

JANUARY 23

IT'S NOT THAT BAD. SOMEBODY OUT
there is hungry right now. So
again, it's not that bad.

JANUARY 24

I AM SICK OF WATCHING YOU PLAY
small! Today you need to take the gloves off
and start swinging. Be brave because I've
got your back. After all, I wrote this book for
you. Now show me I didn't waste our time!

JANUARY 25

YOU ARE NOT IN A JUDGE FREE
zone. They are judging you. Give
them something to talk about.

JANUARY 26

I REALLY DON'T BELIEVE THAT YOU
were supposed to wake up today
just so you could be average.

JANUARY 27

YOU WAKE UP TO A WAR. EVERY single day is a battle. To win this battle you need to either DO something or ELIMINATE something so you can win this fight.

JANUARY 28

WHY ARE YOU HERE COMPLAINING to me that your ship didn't come in? You should be busy swimming out to it.

JANUARY 29

STOP BEING A VICTIM.

Dominance is a mindset.

YOU ARE DOMINANT!

JANUARY 30

"DO YOU KNOW HOW TO BECOME A cage fighter? It's not by reading a book, it's by getting in the freakin' cage!"

- Get Up (Encouraging You To Attack Life) pg. 111

JANUARY 31

IN CASE YOU WEREN'T SURE,

you are good enough.

FEBRUARY 1

#MINDHACK

THE UNIVERSE IS FILLED WITH opposites. This is called the law of polarity. You cannot be a positive person and negative minded at the same time. Be aware and choose wisely.

FEBRUARY 2

WALK AROUND TODAY WITH THE
attitude that you are unstoppable. Oh, and
have your own theme music in your head when
you enter the room, too. Trust me. It's fun.

FEBRUARY 3

THAT FEAR YOU'RE FEELING ABOUT stepping up is temporary. It goes away. The regret you'll have for not stepping up will be with you for the rest of your life. Step up.

FEBRUARY 4

DON'T HATE MONDAY.

Make Monday hate you.

FEBRUARY 5

THE HONEYMOON IS OVER.

Most quit by now and the day to day can be rough. You need to be ON PURPOSE with getting better. Let's stay the course.

FEBRUARY 6

BE CAREFUL WHAT YOU ASK FOR,
you just might get it. You should
have asked for more.

FEBRUARY 7

IT'S EASY TO BE OPTIMISTIC, positive and faithful when things are going great. Being that way when things are going bad is the hardest thing to do. Practice and master this. That is what the champions do.

FEBRUARY 8

SERIOUSLY?

If you're not so jacked that you have another day today, we need to evaluate some things.

FEBRUARY 9

BE GOOD TO YOURSELF.

You get just one of you.

FEBRUARY 10

TODAY IS THE DAY THAT YOU MAKE
the decision to stop being so comfortable.
It's slowly suffocating you.
Challenge yourself today.

FEBRUARY 11

SOMETIMES I FEEL LIKE

I just can't do it. Then I stop listening
to the crap in my head.

FEBRUARY 12

I'M WAITING.

I'm waiting for you to OPEN YOUR FREAKIN' EYES! Look around and start seeing all of this opportunity around you! Let's stop being a victim and let's start getting into activity.

FEBRUARY 13

IF YOU DON'T WHO WILL?

Be the revolution.

It only takes one person to start it.

FEBRUARY 14

IF YOU DON'T ASK THE ANSWER IS
always "No." Start asking and
EXPECT great things.

FEBRUARY 15

NOBODY GETS OUT ALIVE.
We either die up on the bleachers where we criticize, critique and spectate, or we die on the field where we play, learn, experience and really get to live. Don't walk. Hop the fence and RUN onto the field today. Go get your jersey dirty.

FEBRUARY 16

EVERYTHING IS AWESOME,

or everything sucks. You decide.

FEBRUARY 17

YOU HAVE AN ENERGY.

Use it. Light up that room.

FEBRUARY 18

LIVE IN A WAY THAT YOUR FUTURE
self will thank the "right now" you. Take action.

FEBRUARY 19

I KNOW YOU'RE TIRED.
But, so was George Washington and
his troops, and they had no shoes and
walked through snow. Get moving.

FEBRUARY 20

WE ALL GET TIRED. WE ALL GET low. We all fall down. You just can't stay there. GET UP!

FEBRUARY 21

I BELIEVE YOU ARE SPECIAL.

I believe you can do something amazing
that will impact others and elevate
yourself today. Make me right.

FEBRUARY 22

TAKE THE WHEEL

because it's your turn to drive.
This isn't a country song, it's a
direct order. Take the wheel.

FEBRUARY 23

YOU SAID YOU'VE TRIED

everything. I see. Have you tried not giving up?

FEBRUARY 24

THIS IS THE BEST DAY EVER!

Or not. You are actually in control of that.

FEBRUARY 25

LEARN TO HAVE VISION AND
see past the obstacles.

FEBRUARY 26

TRY SMILING FIRST.

It disarms people, diffuses situations
and opens doors. Smile.

FEBRUARY 27

I HAVE A SIMPLE RULE.

Know what you are good at. Know what you are bad at. The thing that you are good at? Do that.

FEBRUARY 28

EVERYBODY WANTS TO BE

successful until they see that success
looks like a lot of hard work.

MARCH 1

#MINDHACK

THOUGHT CONTROL IS IMPERATIVE. Thought control takes discipline. Discipline your thoughts AND emotions because depression cripples and fear paralyzes. You need to put that back in the box and grow mentally strong.

MARCH 2

THIS BOOK IS SUBTITLED
*"*Encouraging You To Attack Life."
It's not "Hit Snooze, Scratch Your Rear
And See What Happens Next." Let's go,
jelly roll. We have galaxies to conquer.

MARCH 3

FROM THE ONES AT THE BOTTOM
to the one at the top, treat all people with
respect. They either expect it, appreciate
it or deserve it. You win with all three.

MARCH 4

GOOD MORNING.

You are doing better than you give
yourself credit for. Keep going.

MARCH 5

CURLED UP IN A BALL ON THE couch covered in a blanket of fear is no way to live. You NEED to take a stand and it all starts with activity.

MARCH 6

ATTACK YOUR GOALS!

They don't just achieve themselves.

Fight for it, already.

MARCH 7

YOUR WORDS ARE POWERFUL.
Be hypersensitive and selective with them.

MARCH 8

IF YOUR REASON FOR NOT GETTING started is because you are afraid of failure, then fear has already won.

MARCH 9

C'MON NOW.

Don't allow yourself to be lazy. Today is the day that you will do something that matters.

MARCH 10

YOU ARE DIFFERENT. EMBRACE that. Embrace your "different." It makes you even more special.

MARCH 11

DO NOT GIVE UP ON MIRACLES.
They happen every single day. Pray.
Speak about the impossible. Believe.

MARCH 12

IT COULD BE WORSE.
You could get punched in the face for a living.
If you are a boxer, it could be even worse
than that. You could have lived during the
time of gladiators. In Rome. Be grateful.

MARCH 13

SOMEBODY WOULD TRADE PLACES

with you in a heartbeat. It's all about perspective.

MARCH 14

STILL HERE?

Most have quit by now. I knew you were different.
I knew you were a winner. Keep pushing.

MARCH 15

EVERY CHAMPION YOU HAVE EVER
seen was once a contender.
They just never gave up.

MARCH 16

EMERSON SAID "A MAN IS WHAT HE thinks about all day long." I think Emerson was right. So if I'm right, you should think good things.

MARCH 17

THAT PEOPLE PLEASING THING ISN'T
working for you. Switch gears.

MARCH 18

DO YOU KNOW HOW
pizza makes people happy? Well, someone
you know needs to be cheered up today.
So, make them happy. Be their pizza.

MARCH 19

EACH DAY YOU ARE EITHER A STEP
closer or farther from your goal. Today,
take actions to step closer.

MARCH 20

THAT LIMIT YOU PUT ON YOURSELF
is false.

MARCH 21

DO YOU KNOW WHAT'S IN THE dark? The dark. Stop being afraid. It's time for you to show courage.

MARCH 22

TRASH IS MEANT TO BE TAKEN OUT,
not kept in your head. You are not a trashcan.
Have clear vision and be on purpose today.

MARCH 23

DO SOMETHING THAT FEELS
uncomfortable today. That's how you grow.

MARCH 24

WHATEVER YOU DO, WORK IT LIKE
your life depends on it. Someday, it might.

MARCH 25

DO WHAT YOU LOVE.

Love what you do. Or, go do something else.

MARCH 26

THOU SHALL NOT GET
comfortable.

MARCH 27

IF YOU WAKE UP FEELING LIKE YOU
don't have a purpose or anything to do today,
go volunteer to help the hungry, the homeless,
hurting children, lonely elderly, or dying veterans.
If you have plans, fit it in somehow anyway.
You'll never be "bored" again in your life.

MARCH 28

YOUR LIFE GOT HARDER? OH.
Congrats. You've been rewarded with an opportunity to grow. You must have leveled up.

MARCH 29

BE THANKFUL FOR EVERYTHING.
Every, little thing. Somebody out
there would kill to be you.

MARCH 30

LOSE YOUR COOL AND YOU LOSE.

MARCH 31

SOME PEOPLE BELIEVE WHAT THEY believe, because they know what they know, and that's that. You'll never change everyone's mind, but you should be okay with that. You do you, boo.

APRIL 1

#MINDHACK

POPULAR ISN'T ALWAYS "RIGHT," and "right" isn't always popular. Don't worry about people's opinions because they'll always have them. Do what you need to do to make things "right."

APRIL 2

FIND YOUR PASSION, FIND YOUR
purpose and you can find your "success."

APRIL 3

WE CAN CREATE OUR OWN PRISON.
We can also create our own key to free
ourselves from that prison. You are
much stronger than you realize.

APRIL 4

ALWAYS ENTER THE ROOM LIKE YOU
have theme music. And, a cape.

APRIL 5

YOU'VE GOT TO BE KIDDING ME.
You need a kick in the rear? You are ALIVE!
What are you waiting for, an invite? Fine. You
are cordially invited to PLAY ALL OUT. Now!

APRIL 6

"I BELIEVE YOU CAN SMASH excuses, too. How? By having zero tolerance. No excuses allowed. Having a no-matter-what mindset."

- Get Up (Encouraging You To Attack Life) pg. 24

APRIL 7

BE THE FIRST TO SHOW UP
and the last to leave.

APRIL 8

JUST OUTWORK EVERYONE ELSE.

The real competition is the one in the mirror.

APRIL 9

THERE ARE ALWAYS GOING TO BE
critics. Don't worry about proving.
Focus on improving.

APRIL 10

DO YOU REMEMBER THE GUY

who quit? Me either. Let's go.

APRIL 11

WORK IT LIKE YOU MEAN IT.

Win, lose or draw, make sure that everyone
knows that you are to be respected.

APRIL 12

YOUR EGO IS BLINDING YOU FROM growth. And, if you just dismissed this, unfortunately you've made me right.

APRIL 13

IS IT EASIER TO PROCRASTINATE
now, or live with regret for the
rest of your life? GET UP!

APRIL 14

IF YOU ONLY REALIZED

how special you really are...

APRIL 15

STOP WASTING YOUR TIME.

Get at it like you mean it.

APRIL 16

THIS IS A PRETTY SIMPLE FORMULA.
To be the best, first you need to be great. To be great, you need to be good. To get good, you may need to grow through a phase of bad. And, to be bad, you need to start. Get started.

APRIL 17

IT DOESN'T GET DONE

by thinking about it. Get into activity!

APRIL 18

RANDOMLY REMIND SOMEONE THAT you love them today. You're not promised later.

APRIL 19

DIG DEEPER. WHAT? YOU NEED A better quote? You want more? Maybe you are hoping for a magic bean or something? It's inside of you. DIG. DEEPER.

APRIL 20

DON'T JUST MOVE. MOVE WITH purpose. Rip through the finish line! How? End today better than how you started it.

APRIL 21

I HAVE TWO QUESTIONS.
First, if this was your last day ever,
would you approach it differently?
Second, who said it's not? Go hard.

APRIL 22

SUCCESS DOESN'T SLEEP IN.

Wakey, wakey. Time to freakin' WIN.

APRIL 23

DON'T GIVE UP.

Walt Disney was told he had no imagination. Beethoven was told he was awful at composing. The Beatles were told that they had no future in the music business. Screw the critics. People's opinions do NOT define you. Keep pushing forward.

APRIL 24

WHEN IN DOUBT, SWEAT IT OUT.
We weren't meant to just sit or go through
emotions. Get in shape. You will feel so good after
working out. It's your health. Pay now or pay later.

APRIL 25

THEY TRY TO BREAK US
every single day. Not today, yo. You
are STRONG. Go rip it to shreds.

APRIL 26

EVERY SINGLE TIME YOU WASTE
time thinking about it, somebody else
is making time and going for it.

APRIL 27

THAT DREAM IN YOUR MIND

is only a dream until you start working for it.

APRIL 28

FIGHT OR QUIT.

It's really up to you.

APRIL 29

TAKE CHARGE
and YOU set the pace.

APRIL 30

PREDICT YOUR FUTURE

by CREATING it. Don't just sit back and
let things be dictated to you.

MAY 1

#MINDHACK

SOMETIMES GOD BLOCKS THE GOOD
so you can receive the great. Be thankful if
you don't always get exactly what you want.
The key is to be aware of and looking for the
blessing that you are supposed to receive.

MAY 2

IF THEY TOLD YOU IT WAS EASY
they lied to you. But trust me,
it's worth it. Go get it.

MAY 3

GOOD THINGS COME
to those who...refuse to quit.

MAY 4

AT THE END OF THIS YEAR, YOU
will want to reflect back and be proud
of something you've accomplished. This
is a reminder that that "something"
will not happen randomly.

MAY 5

BECOME BIGGER
than your problems. Grow.

MAY 6

STAY HUNGRY.

Don't you dare get complacent
and soft with your goals.

MAY 7

YOU ARE THE LAWNMOWER AND
everything else is the grass. Time to mow.

MAY 8

SHOW UP.

SCREW UP.

GROW UP.

HUSTLE.

MAY 9

WHEN YOU START TO FEEL
stressed, look around and realize that you
are blessed. Perspective and gratitude
will do wonders for your mental health.

MAY 10

PEOPLE'S PERCEPTION OF ME
doesn't matter to me. People's perception of you
shouldn't matter to you, either. Slay in your lane.

MAY 11

TAKE A BREATH.

Appreciate things.

You are surrounded by beauty.

MAY 12

THERE IS SERIOUSLY NO SUBSTITUTE
for your attitude. It can kick open
doors or slam them shut.

MAY 13

YOU CAN'T SAY THE RIGHT THING
to the wrong person. Stop holding back!

MAY 14

SICK, RIDICULOUS, UNAPOLOGETIC,
relentless work ethic is empowering.
It wins. Go outwork everybody.

MAY 15

YOU CAN ALWAYS REINVENT. DECIDE
that your "prime" is now. Make
these days your "Glory Days."

MAY 16

WHEN SOMEONE IS SPEAKING TO ME
and makes me feel like I am the only one in
the room, it makes me feel special. That's not
something that I forget. Go make someone
feel special when you speak to them today.

MAY 17

TODAY YOU SHOULD ACTUALLY
believe in yourself.

MAY 18

YOU DON'T HAVE TO FALL OFF OF A
cliff to know that it hurts. Pay attention
and learn from the mistakes of others
without having to pay the price.

MAY 19

ENVISION WHAT YOU WANT TO BE
remembered for and go do THAT.

MAY 20

HAVE THE HIGHEST EXPECTATIONS
and accountability for yourself first. This
will raise everybody's game around you.

MAY 21

FEELING OVERWHELMED? DON'T look at the whole thing. Take just one step today.

MAY 22

KEEP LEARNING. BE A MASTER
novice. If you are a mouse in a maze
and you get the cheese every time, get
a new maze. You've outgrown it.

MAY 23

I'M GOING TO SAY THIS ONCE. WE
don't live twice. Make it count NOW.

MAY 24

GROWTH IS SO IMPORTANT.
Start with want. The emotion of wanting
to get better is powerful. Picture yourself
with your heroes who inspire you. Dream
about becoming friends with the people
you currently look up to. Desire that and
work to better yourself with growth.

MAY 25

HOPE AND FAITH

are recession proof. Positivity is free.
Invest in those commodities.

MAY 26

IS THIS A JOKE? SERIOUSLY?

Stop waiting for the perfect time, or
until you get better, or when the freakin'
planets align or whatever you have
going on in that head. LET'S GO!!!

MAY 27

WHEN YOU DWELL ON INFERIORITY
and failure, expect to become inferior and fail.
If you focus on high standards and success,
you will raise your standards and can expect
to attract opportunity and success.

MAY 28

THE REAL LEADERS, THE GREAT
ones, usually arrive first and leave last.
That's why I keep advising you to do it.

MAY 29

LIFE IS A LOT LIKE BASEBALL;
three strikes and you're out. Or maybe life
is like football; you get four downs. It could
be like boxing; twelve rounds? Maybe it's
like bowling; three hundred pins. How about
this? Let's stop putting limits on life and
just live it to the fullest. Keep going.

MAY 30

DON'T JUST SHOW UP.

Show up with a plan and with PURPOSE.

It makes such a difference.

MAY 31

A STRENGTH IS KNOWING YOUR
weakness, and a weakness is not
knowing your strength. Learn who
you are and run hard with that.

JUNE 1

#MINDHACK

EVERY SINGLE TIME YOU HOLD back, you are disappointing others who need the benefit of the gift you were created and blessed with. If you sing, sing! If you build, build! If you lead, then stop thinking about it and go lead! You were meant for MORE than what you are doing right now.

JUNE 2

UNDERSTAND THAT YOU WEREN'T
created to live with a spirit of fear.

JUNE 3

HELLO, SUNSHINE. GO DOMINATE!

JUNE 4

IF YOU DON'T WANT TO BE LIKE 'em, don't hang with 'em. Surround yourself with those that you aspire to be like.

JUNE 5

IT'S HARD TO ENJOY THE JOURNEY
when the journey isn't enjoyable, right?
Right. So, find SOMETHING that you LOVE
about the journey. Open your mind.

JUNE 6

WE AS A SOCIETY ARE CONSTANTLY pointed to the competitive aspect. Lose that. Tune more into your creative side. Watch how things can drastically change for the better.

JUNE 7

ALWAYS GIVE THE BENEFIT OF THE doubt and try not to judge. You don't know what battle that person is fighting.

JUNE 8

ALL YOU HAVE TO GIVE IS 100%.

If not, somebody else will win because they will.

JUNE 9

THE DEFINITION OF REALISTIC IS "Having or showing a sensible and practical idea of what can be achieved or expected." I think the definition of realistic should be "Having an excuse prepared for expected failure." I think it's time you stop being realistic and you start getting delusional so you can start getting past your limits.

JUNE 10

POTENTIAL JUST MEANS THAT YOU really haven't done anything yet. Stop having potential and start sweating so you can start having results.

JUNE 11

BESIDES THIS BOOK, YOU'VE
opened two other gifts this morning;
your eyes. Be thankful, praise God and
go be a blessing to someone today.

JUNE 12

STOP BEING ENTITLED AND
offended so easily. Life is tough. Wear a cup.

JUNE 13

DO WHAT MOST DON'T.

Be mature enough to step away from your emotions and take a hard look at WHY you are not where you want to be. Now, be brave enough to go fix it.

JUNE 14

YOU ARE GOING TO MAKE MISTAKES.
As a matter of fact, you are going to make
a ton of them. The ultimate mistake would
be to not learn from them. Keep your eyes
open and pay attention to the lesson.

JUNE 15

REFUSE TO LOSE.
That's not a t-shirt, a meme or a
slogan. That's a mindset.

JUNE 16

WHEN YOU FEEL OVERWHELMED
because you have "too much on your plate,"
remember that you have a plate in the first place.

JUNE 17

OVERDRESS.

Never apologize for looking great.

JUNE 18

TOO MANY PEOPLE WILL SHUT down before they even try. They get overwhelmed with a big picture of a long journey before they ever experience the beauty of starting with a small step. Take your first small step today and create your journey.

JUNE 19

TODAY, YOU WILL BE IMPACTFUL!

JUNE 20

LIFE IS LIKE A SMORGASBORD AND we all gotta eat. How will you know what you do or don't like if you always have the same thing? Try something totally new and out of character for you today. Go eat, baby!

JUNE 21

QUIT ANXIETY.

IGNORE DRAMA.

RISE ABOVE ALL OF IT.

JUNE 22

LOOK AT ALL THOSE PEOPLE WHO
dropped their New Year Resolutions six months
ago as you keep reading and keep getting
better. You have tenacity and I am impressed!

JUNE 23

YOU PUT TOO MUCH UNNECESSARY
pressure on yourself. Give yourself
a mental break today.

JUNE 24

WHAT? YOU HAVE PEOPLE WHO
want you to fail? You must be doing great. If you
have haters, you are probably making an impact.

JUNE 25

THE BEST PRESENT IS TO BE
present. Be on your toes and pay attention today.

JUNE 26

WHAT IS THE "BULLY" IN YOUR LIFE
that keeps holding you down? Sometimes,
you just need to go pick a fight with the bully.
Charge your Goliath and go rip it's head off.

JUNE 27

"LET'S STOP BEING LAZY.
Let's stop being comfy. Let's stop being scared. Let's get out of our own head and out of our own way. Let's start a revolution of inspiration. Let's get at it! Get hungry, stay hungry and start hunting."

- Get Up (Encouraging You To Attack Life) pg. 118

JUNE 28

THIS IS A VERY NOISY WORLD.
On social media and in person, everyone -
EVERYONE - is competing for attention.
GIVE them the attention that they crave.
Then, you'll automatically get yours.

JUNE 29

REMEMBER THAT THEY LAUGHED at you. Remember that they didn't take you seriously. Know that they are laughing now. Use this as fuel to drive you so you can make sure that you are never a punchline again.

JUNE 30

YOU ONLY HAVE SO MANY SLEEPS,
breaths and days left. Sleep soundly.
Breathe deeply. Live each day like you
mean it. Your life is precious.

JULY 1

THOUGHTS BECOME THINGS. YOUR
belief will create facts. Be hypersensitive,
aware and purposeful with your
thoughts, words and emotions.

JULY 2

ALL IT TAKES IS ONE GOOD SHOT.

Take yours.

JULY 3

DO YOU WANT TO WIN? THEN DON'T
focus on winning. Focus on the work. Start DOING
all the mundane, ugly, unpleasant tasks that
others aren't willing to do. Get your hands dirty
and start doing what it takes. Then you'll win.

JULY 4

IT'S REALLY TRUE. IF YOU'RE NOT growing, you are dying. So what are you going to do to grow today? It can even be watching YouTube, just make sure you watch something that stimulates your mind, not sedates it.

JULY 5

THE UNIVERSE RESPONDS TO THE
BRAVE. You must take a stand and
do something. Be BRAVE today.

JULY 6

COMFORTABLE WON'T IMPRESS

anyone. It really isn't something to brag about.

JULY 7

I'M NOT WORRIED THAT YOU AREN'T
winning. I'm worried that you're thinking
of quitting because you aren't winning.

JULY 8

MAYBE YOU'VE BEEN TOO
comfortable?

JULY 9

I'M REALLY NOT CRAZY.
I just continue to believe in you, even
when you stop believing in yourself.

JULY 10

FIND YOUR WINDOW OF
opportunity. Open the door to opportunity.
If there's no window and you can't find the
door, screw it. Smash down the whole freakin'
wall and create your own opportunity.

JULY 11

IF YOU CHOOSE TO NOT KEEP A
positive attitude through tough times,
understand that you will still will have
tough times; you'll just be negative too.

JULY 12

THE GREATEST LEADERS HAVE BEEN
defined by their actions during moments of
adversity. Seize your moment of adversity
as an opportunity to do something great.

JULY 13

GO HELP SOMEONE IN NEED WHO IS
less fortunate than you. Your problems will shrink.

JULY 14

DID YOU EVER NOTICE THAT WHEN
you multitask, you seem to get a little bit of
everything done? Did you also notice that
when you focus on one task in particular,
you dominate? Just pointing out that maybe
you should be specific and focus today.

JULY 15

MY FATHER WOULD TELL ME

"Don't work hard. Work smart." I'm introducing version 2.0. "Work hard at working smart."

JULY 16

QUIT FREAKING CRYING ALREADY.
Stand up and fight!

JULY 17

VAN GOGH ONCE SAID

"I dream my painting then I paint my dream."
Visualize what you want and then go create that.

JULY 18

BE THANKFUL FOR ANYONE OR anything that has ever beaten you up, held you back or knocked you down. These are the contributors to the amazing story you will tell after your comeback. Each loss is an experience and each setback paves the way for your comeback.

JULY 19

HEAD UP AND KEEP THOSE FEET
moving. You're not allowed to stay down.

JULY 20

PEOPLE WILL DISAPPOINT YOU.

Learn to forgive. It will make you powerful.

JULY 21

GOD HAS A PLAN. STAY FAITHFUL.

It happens in His time, not ours.

JULY 22

YOU SAY YOU'VE FAILED.
I say you were brave enough to
go for it. Fix how you think.

JULY 23

EVERYBODY NEEDS A BREAK.

Don't forget to take one. Don't forget to give one.

JULY 24

I BELIEVE PREPARATION IS THE
difference between good or great,
success or failure. If you just show up
to "wing it," we are going to know.

JULY 25

ENOUGH IS ENOUGH.

Today it's your turn.

YOU take control.

JULY 26

MOST PEOPLE WILL WAKE UP AND
see how things go. They'll allow things
to happen to them, situations to dictate
and give their control over to someone or
something else. Don't be like everybody. YOU
take control. YOU set the pace. Be a boss.

JULY 27

YOU DESERVE MORE. GO GET IT.

It's not gonna come to you by accident.

JULY 28

TODAY DO SOMETHING

to pay it forward or give back.

JULY 29

IF YOU BELIEVE YOU CAN'T,
then you can't. Retrain yourself.
Start thinking you can.

JULY 30

LET'S HAVE SOME FUN.
Do something today that you would never dream
of doing because it scares you to death. That's
right. LEAP out of your comfort zone. I dare you.

JULY 31

IT'S NOT TOO LATE.

You can start today. That change happens
with you choosing. You are so in control.

AUGUST 1
#MINDHACK

WE ALL HAVE THE SAME 24 HOURS.
Eight is for rest. Eight is for work. Eight is up to
you. We fill that last eight with the shows that we
watch, the social media that we scroll, the sports
that we follow, and reality that we run away from.
Try an experiment. Take seven hours and forty
five minutes for sports, shows and pleasure. Use
fifteen minutes - everyday - for self-fulfilling
personal growth. Check back in a month. See
what kind of person you are becoming.

AUGUST 2

STOP SAYING THOSE FILTHY WORDS
like "can't," and "impossible," or "realistic."
Your words have power so watch your mouth.

AUGUST 3

THERE'S ENOUGH SUNSHINE FOR
everyone to get a tan. Don't hate.
Appreciate. We all can win.

AUGUST 4

I BELIEVE IN FORGIVENESS,
second chances and comebacks. Forgive
others. Forgive yourself. Take that first
step and start your comeback today.

AUGUST 5

FEAR IS A LIAR. GO DO IT.

AUGUST 6

IF YOU'RE INTO PEOPLE PLEASING, you shouldn't expect success. You should expect a few more "likes" on your Facebook wall.

AUGUST 7

UNFAIR OR NOT, WITHIN SECONDS
you will be judged on how you dress. Look sharp.

AUGUST 8

"TROUBLE" IS ONLY ONE'S
perception
of circumstance. I'm not saying cause
"trouble." I'm saying push the envelope.

AUGUST 9

IF YOU'RE GOING TO BOTHER WITH
putting in all that work, you might as
well be great. Have big vision.

AUGUST 10

"CAN'T" IS FALSE. IT'S WEAK.

Find a way. Just find a way.

AUGUST 11

LIFE IS LIKE A HANDSHAKE.
Take it too lightly and you are perceived
weak. Do it too hard and you seem to be
overcompensating. Firm is good. Be firm.

AUGUST 12

NOT "FEELING IT TODAY?"

Aw, I hear ya, buddy. Why don't you go have a cookie. On second thought, GET UP! LET'S GO!!

AUGUST 13

JUST SMILE ANYWAY.

AUGUST 14

I'M BEGGING YOU TO GO OUTSIDE of the lines. Rewrite the rules. Don't be defined by other people's limits.

AUGUST 15

YOUR PAST DOES NOT DEFINE YOU,
unless you keep living in it. Move on.

AUGUST 16

NEVER FORGET THAT YOU ARE
unique, talented and beautiful with
your own special gift. Your job is to
share that gift with the world.

AUGUST 17

WHEN SOMEONE TELLS YOU THAT
something you want to succeed in is "impossible,"
that is them putting their limits on you.
That's cute. Now, go make them apologize.

AUGUST 18

ENOUGH IS ENOUGH ALREADY.

Take that pain and use it as fuel.

AUGUST 19

TODAY YOU HAVE A DECISION to make, and there are only two options. Today you choose whether you get better or you get worse. That's it. Choose.

AUGUST 20

EVERYONE HAS A DIFFERENT STORY.
That's why you can't compare apples to oranges,
and you shouldn't compare yourself with others.

AUGUST 21

OPEN DOORS FOR OTHERS,
literally and figuratively.

AUGUST 22

WHEN YOU GET HIT,

hit back. Twice. Harder.

AUGUST 23

THE "OVERNIGHT" HOUSEHOLD
name superstars have toiled for years in
darkness quietly scratching and grinding when
it wasn't glamorous. Have some patience.

AUGUST 24

SKEPTICISM WILL NOT JUST KEEP you broke, it will make you broke. Just like the radio pioneers who weren't impressed with the television, or the horse and buggy riders who wanted nothing to do with the automobiles, and all those people who never pay attention when a good opportunity comes along. Be open minded.

AUGUST 25

DON'T WORRY ABOUT THE FUTURE.
Work on RIGHT NOW and the future
will take care of itself.

AUGUST 26

YOU DON'T LOSE.
You win or you learn.

AUGUST 27

DON'T EXPECT OR ASSUME anything. Always be prepared. This will save you from headaches.

AUGUST 28

EVERY SINGLE TIME YOU DECIDE
to take a short cut, take a break or do it
"next time," the other guy is winning.

AUGUST 29

GOOD MORNING, CUPCAKE.

It's time to take control. Go get it.

AUGUST 30

"SAY WHAT YOU MEAN
and mean what you say."

- David D. Hayford Jr.
(Dad)

AUGUST 31

STOP TRYING TO FIT IN.

You weren't meant for that.

SEPTEMBER 1

#MINDHACK

IF YOU ARE GOING TO ACHIEVE success, you need to not see where you are, but where you are going. Do NOT let your present circumstances squash your future opportunities. Vision is crucial.

SEPTEMBER 2

MAKE THEM DRAG YOU OUT;

kicking and screaming.

SEPTEMBER 3

EXPECT PEOPLE TO BE HAPPY TO see you today. Expect that today everything will go right for you. Expect people to say "Yes" to you. Today, expect to win.

SEPTEMBER 4

YOU KNOW EXACTLY WHAT TO DO.

Go do it already!

SEPTEMBER 5

REFUSE TO WORRY. WORRY IS FEAR and fear is a liar. "Fear" = False Evidence Appearing Real. Screw fear.

SEPTEMBER 6

THERE'S ALWAYS GOING TO BE
somebody that just doesn't like you.
Why are you trying to please them?

SEPTEMBER 7

KEEP READING. SOONER OR LATER

I'm going to get you to believe
that you are a beast.

SEPTEMBER 8

GOOD MORNING.

Now go rip through everything in your way.

SEPTEMBER 9

ATTITUDE IS ABSOLUTELY
everything. Go get one and work it like
Conor McGregor in an octagon.

SEPTEMBER
10

BE THE ONE THEY TALK ABOUT.

SEPTEMBER 11

STOP. HOLDING. BACK.

There are people counting on you!

SEPTEMBER 12

I JUST WANTED TO TELL YOU THAT
you will run into some problems today.
I also wanted to advise you to rip them
to shreds when they show up.

SEPTEMBER 13

I AM TERRIBLE AT MAKING pancakes. That's why I DJ. I'm better at it. Go do more of what you're good at.

SEPTEMBER 14

DO YOU KNOW WHICH ATHLETES have highlight reels? The ones who put the work in before anybody was ever watching.

SEPTEMBER 15

SOME PEOPLE SAY THEY DON'T MIX business and pleasure. I think if you have a business that doesn't bring you pleasure, you should get a new business. Love it or leave it.

SEPTEMBER 16

YOU KNOW THAT THING THAT KEEPS hanging over your head and bothering you? Yeah. That. Today I want you to run hard at it. Seriously. I don't want you to just face it, I want you attacking that and putting an end to it. Be the bully.

SEPTEMBER 17

CONGRATULATIONS, SUNSHINE.

You woke up. That means more opportunity!

SEPTEMBER 18

EXCUSES ARE FOR LOSERS. YOU ARE a winner. No excuses.

SEPTEMBER 19

GO ON THE OFFENSE. THAT'S RIGHT.

I just told you to get offensive.

Go make some moves.

SEPTEMBER 20

REMEMBER THAT THING THAT YOU were really worried about like twelve years ago? Me neither. Stop worrying and start living.

SEPTEMBER 21

YOU WANT RESPECT? THEN YOU can't be a prima donna. Roll up your sleeves and take on the dirty work that everyone else is afraid to do. Step up and you become the leader.

SEPTEMBER
22

SOMEBODY TOOK THE SAME
problem you have and won with it big
time. Stop having limitations.

SEPTEMBER 23

ONCE YOU READ THIS, CLOSE THIS
book. Something in your life needs
to get done. Do it now.

SEPTEMBER 24

I WISH YOU COULD SEE YOURSELF
the way I see you. You would play
to win. You'd be fearless.

SEPTEMBER 25

IMPULSIVE CAN BE FUN AND
emotions are short lived. Have the
discipline to not make permanent decisions
off of your temporary emotions.

SEPTEMBER 26

THOMAS EDISON IS CREDITED WITH discovering the lightbulb. His famous quote reads "I have not failed. I have just found 10,000 ways that won't work." Just think. Some of us quit before we ever get started.

SEPTEMBER 27

PLANNING IS GREAT, BUT IT ONLY goes so far. There will never be a "perfect" time. Get started.

SEPTEMBER 28

SOMEWHERE, SOMEONE IS
counting on you. Give your best effort.

SEPTEMBER
29

"COMFORTABLE DOESN'T GROW,
comfortable doesn't achieve, and
comfortable never wins."

*- Get Up (Encouraging
You To Attack Life) pg. 53*

SEPTEMBER
30

CHAMPIONS DO NOT HAVE
"office hours."

OCTOBER 1

#MINDHACK

ALL OF YOUR SUSTAINED, consecutive thoughts add up to the type of person you become. It is vital to nurture and pour into yourself daily so you can create positive momentum. You have a long journey.

OCTOBER 2

YOU ARE WORTH IT. YOU ARE
special.
You are needed. You are somebody's whole world.

OCTOBER 3

DO NOT BE SATISFIED.

Roll those sleeves up.

There's a lot more in your tank.

OCTOBER 4

THE DECISIONS YOU MAKE TODAY
are what people will remember
about you tomorrow.

OCTOBER 5

WE ARE SET UP TO LOSE. THIS world is noisy, there are a zillion distractions and your phone is your enemy. Want success? Stop scrolling, swiping and binging. Your focus is vital.

OCTOBER 6

YOUR PRESENT CIRCUMSTANCE AND current situation is not your final destination.

OCTOBER 7

FALL IN LOVE WITH THE HARD
work that everybody else shies away from. That's
how you become a legend. Think about it.

OCTOBER 8

THAT DREAM? FIGHT FOR IT.

OCTOBER 9

WHEN A CHILD IS LEARNING TO walk and she falls down fifty times, she doesn't think to herself "Maybe this isn't for me." She gets back up for the fifty first.

OCTOBER 10

YOU'VE SEEN ME WRITE "WHEN YOU get hit, hit back. Twice. Harder." Do that. But, this time add one more for good measure.

OCTOBER 11

SO MANY WANT TO WEAR THE
varsity jacket, but they don't want to go
to team practice. There is no substitute
or way around that hard work.

OCTOBER 12

YOU WEREN'T PUT HERE TO JUST
exist.
Go make a difference.

OCTOBER 13

THEY AREN'T GOING TO REMEMBER
your name if you just fall back
like everybody else. GET UP!

OCTOBER 14

QUIT COMPLAINING.
Look around and see how blessed you actually
are. Become a solution, not a problem.

OCTOBER 15

I THINK AN AWESOME GOAL TO
have is to work it so hard that you no longer
need to introduce yourself when you show up.

OCTOBER 16

STOP KEEPING SCORE.

Nobody owes you anything.

OCTOBER 17

THINK ABOUT IT.

The energy you are putting out is exactly what you are getting back. If you want to change what you're getting, change what you're giving.

OCTOBER 18

MOST PEOPLE WILL VIEW A problem or an obstacle and claim "This can't be done." The good entrepreneurs, the world's greatest innovators and the minds who achieve will view those same issues and ask "How can this be done?" Start asking the right questions.

OCTOBER 19

TO ACHIEVE IT, YOU MUST BELIEVE
it. If you don't believe it, how can you achieve it?

OCTOBER 20

THIS MAY HURT FEELINGS BUT IT needs to be said. Every single time you spend your time blaming someone else, you waste your breath, bring a negative energy, project weakness and look small. Man up, shut up and get better so there doesn't need to be blame.

OCTOBER 21

YOU CAN. REALLY.

OCTOBER 22

WE'RE ALL OUT HERE TRYING TO
figure this life thing out. Be patient with others
today, even if they don't deserve it. They
may need your grace more than you think.

OCTOBER 23

IF YOU WANT WHAT THE WINNERS have, then you need to do what the winners do. They don't win by accident.

OCTOBER 24

IF YOU DIDN'T PUT IN THE TIME,
and if you didn't do the work, you
shouldn't expect the results.

OCTOBER 25

DISCIPLINE ISN'T JUST SOMETHING that rhymes with citizen. It is what gets things done. Use it today.

OCTOBER 26

ADVERSITY WILL HAPPEN.
HOW you handle it will define YOU.

OCTOBER 27

I JUST WANT YOU TO KNOW THAT
we have spent the past three hundred mornings
together. I appreciate you and I hope I bring you
inspiration and joy. Today go appreciate someone
and tell them why. You'll make their day.

OCTOBER 28

THAT PERSON AT THE TOP OF THE
mountain wasn't magically brought
there by a hot air balloon.

OCTOBER 29

IT'S NOT ALL PUPPIES AND
rainbows, but it's not all doom
and gloom either. Smile.

OCTOBER 30

I KNOW YOU'VE MISSED A FEW
days. That's okay. I'm here for you.
Now, catch up and remember that
today is a great day. Keep going.

OCTOBER 31

WHY ARE YOU SO FOCUSED ON
what others think? How's that been
working for you? Do your thing.

NOVEMBER 1

#MINDHACK

DO YOU KNOW HOW YOU FEEL LIKE you "just can't catch a break" and how you "just can't win?" You're right. You attract that energy onto yourself. Start acting, thinking, talking and telling yourself that you are a winner, and you will be.

NOVEMBER 2

NORMAL IS BORING.

Be different. As a matter of fact, embrace it.

NOVEMBER 3

LET GO OF THAT STRESS.

Just choose to be happy today. It won't be easy, because we are all trained to lean toward the negative. But, let it go. Be happy.

NOVEMBER 4

YOU DIDN'T COME THIS FAR

just to come this far.

NOVEMBER 5

MOST PEOPLE SLEEPWALK THROUGH life. I'm telling you if you are not living and growing, you are dying. Keep your feet moving and get involved. You are needed.

NOVEMBER 6

I FIND THE IDEA OF REGRET TO BE
terrifying. It should scare you, too. Not regret
for what was done, but regret for what was
never tried. Play all out while you still can.

NOVEMBER 7

SHOW TODAY NO MERCY AND BRING it to it's knees. Or, let it bring you to yours. Fight!

NOVEMBER 8

EVERYTHING UP TO THIS POINT HAS
NOT been wasted time. Everything up to
this point has made you one experienced
professional. Now, I have a question about your
experience. What are you going to do with it?

NOVEMBER 9

IF YOU WANT SOMETHING, GO GET IT. The fairy tale stuff is great in a Disney movie. This is real life. Go get it.

NOVEMBER 10

TODAY YOU WILL BE ON PURPOSE.

All day. On purpose.

NOVEMBER 11

"...FEED THAT MOST POWERFUL
asset - your mind. What you tell yourself -
how you currently view yourself makes
all the difference in the world."

- Get Up (Encouraging
You To Attack Life) pg. 46

NOVEMBER 12

YOU ARE STRONGER THAN YOU

think. I can't wait until you realize this!

NOVEMBER 13

DON'T ASK. DEMAND.

NOVEMBER 14

EVERYBODY HAS AN OPINION.
So do I. My opinion is that I don't care
about their opinion. I do my own thing.
Feel free to borrow that one.

NOVEMBER 15

DON'T CHOOSE THE HERD.

Don't choose to be unimportant. Become a factor. Stand up. Stand out. Make an impact.

NOVEMBER 16

IN THE PAST I'VE HEARD MENTORS
say "Activity fixes everything."
They were right. Get moving.

NOVEMBER 17

I AM SOOO ABOUT YOU PLAYING hard now. In the future, when you look back at tomorrow you'll see a bright past.

NOVEMBER 18

EVERY FIFTEEN SECONDS THERE
are distractions in our lives. They are keeping
us from our greater goals. We must shut them
out with purpose so we can have time to focus.

NOVEMBER 19

IF YOU WANT SOMETHING - AND I
mean really, really want something, you have
to do more than just want it. You need to work
it, eat it, breathe it, walk, talk, daydream,
and obsess over it until you own it!

NOVEMBER 20

LUCK, CHANCE AND COINCIDENCE IS garbage. This happened for a reason.

NOVEMBER 21

IT'S NOVEMBER.

Who's relentless in November? You are.

Be relentless. I promise it pays off.

NOVEMBER 22

STOP WASTING YOUR TIME.

It's precious. Make it count!

NOVEMBER 23

TODAY MAKE A DECISION TO LOOK people in the eyes when you speak with them. Look hard into their eyes. Watch how you become more confident, and how they will give you more respect.

NOVEMBER 24

I HAVE ADVICE FOR YOU.

I'm going to advise you to "get up,"
and I am encouraging you to ATTACK
life today. Good advice, right?

NOVEMBER 25

BAD COMPANY CAN CORRUPT GOOD
character. Be selective. Be a snob. Have a
high standard. You owe it to the future you.

NOVEMBER 26

WHEN I SEE BOASTING, I SEE weakness. Don't feel like you have to compare with them, because you don't. They are weak. Being confident within yourself should be sufficient enough. Be strong.

NOVEMBER 27

GET BACK IN THE TRENCHES

immediately. It's where all the battles are won.

NOVEMBER 28

IF YOU WOKE UP THIS MORNING
and are able to read this, you're
doing alright. Be thankful.

NOVEMBER 29

TODAY YOU WON'T BE A TAKER.
Today you will be a giver. What will you give?
You will give your time, give your love, give
your money or give your strength. You choose.
Today you will give because someone needs it.
You can't take it with you when you're gone.

NOVEMBER 30

OVERSHOOT WITH YOUR STANDARD

so at the very least you hit your target.
Act like the leader you are.

DECEMBER 1

#MINDHACK

ANY QUANTUM PHYSICIST WILL affirm the law of attraction where like attracts like. Just because you don't understand it doesn't mean you should reject it. You may not understand how, but you know when you hit the light switch the lights come on. The law of attraction is real. Be on purpose with what you are attracting.

DECEMBER 2

SOME PEOPLE MAKE EXCUSES.

Some people win. Choose wisely.

DECEMBER 3

I'VE HEARD THIS SO MANY TIMES
and it always rings true.
What you allow will continue.

DECEMBER 4

I KNOW IT'S TOUGH,

but so are you. Let's go.

DECEMBER 5

YOU CANNOT MOVE FORWARD WHEN you are holding back. Stop the scarcity mindset. Thinking small does NOT serve you. Today, you play all out.

DECEMBER 6

I BELIEVE YOUR ENERGY REALLY does matter. It's primal. It matters with kids. It matter with animals. Why would it be any different for you?

DECEMBER 7

THERE ARE SO MANY TIMES WHEN I
could choose to focus on my shortcomings.
And, believe me, there are many. But, I don't.
And, I can't. Neither can you. We can't afford
to. Life is too short. We need to continue to
push forward and go with what we're good at.

DECEMBER 8

JOHN LENNON SAID "EVERYTHING
will be okay in the end. If it's not
okay, it's not the end."

DECEMBER 9

EGO? IT SHOWS WEAKNESS.
It's a turnoff. Confidence? Very powerful.
Commanding. It attracts. Be conscious of
dropping the ego and be open to being open.

DECEMBER 10

EASY IS WORTHLESS.

Your sweat means something.

DECEMBER 11

YES. I HAVE SCARS.

They are magnificent. Just like yours. They are a history lesson, they demand respect, and there are not any other like them in the world.

DECEMBER 12

GET YOUR HEAD RIGHT.

They need you out there today. Go be
the difference maker that you are.

DECEMBER 13

NOT IF, BUT WHEN SOMEBODY IS
abrasive, a jerk, or just giving you a hard
time today, remember this: hurt people
hurt people. Give them a pass.

DECEMBER 14

YOU ARE NEVER "DONE."

Don't be satisfied. Be insatiable.

DECEMBER 15

YOU HAVE TO BE CLEAR WITH YOUR goal, dream and vision. You need to be specific. You wouldn't send a message to someone with a bunch of mixed up words. You would be very specific with your message so it could be understood. Be very specific with your goals. They need to be understood.

DECEMBER 16

STOP BEING SO JADED!

It's not as bad as you think. Start looking
for the possibilities and opportunities.

DECEMBER 17

YOUR MIND IS POWERFUL.
If you don't control it, it will
control you. Be on purpose.

DECEMBER 18

THE THING YOU ARE SHYING AWAY from the most could cause your biggest breakthrough. May I suggest slaying it?

DECEMBER 19

THEY ASKED ME IF I COULD DO more. They said "Raise your hand as high as you can." I did. Then they said "Now, raise it a little bit higher." I did. Then they said to me "See? You CAN do more."

DECEMBER 20

YOU GET A BRAND NEW

opportunity each day. It's called morning.

DECEMBER 21

DID YOU EVER HEAR

"Busy people are busy for a reason?" Well they are. And, they may always be. But, there is a distinct difference between busy and productive. Choose productive.

DECEMBER 22

SOMETIMES YOU FORGET HOW
special you really are. You are special.

DECEMBER 23

FROM THE BIBLE TO EVERY HISTORY book, so many of the greatest leaders have felt unworthy for their calling. Believe in yourself. You can be great.

DECEMBER 24

KEEP YOUR HEAD UP.

Keep your faith. Keep moving forward.

DECEMBER 25

THAT PEACE ON EARTH THING?

It starts inside of you.

DECEMBER 26

TAKE A DISH AND BREAK IT INTO little pieces on the floor. Now, tell it that you're sorry. Is it still broken or did it piece back together? Be aware of how you treat others today. Our words and actions are powerful. Let's try not to break anyone.

DECEMBER 27

I AM NOT ONE TO TELL YOU TO
quit. But, if you don't have a passion
for what you do, go do something else.
You are wasting all of our time.

DECEMBER 28

IF YOU CHANGE NOTHING,
nothing will change.

DECEMBER 29

"IGNITE OTHERS.
Welcome the journey. Enjoy the growth.
Appreciate the struggle. Screw the critics. Allow
yourself to fly...stop stopping yourself so you can
start doing you and live the life that you deserve."

- Get Up (Encouraging
You To Attack Life) pg. 92

DECEMBER 30

YOU ARE NOT QUALIFIED TO BE A leader if you are not willing to serve like a servant. Don't be too important for anything.

DECEMBER 31

YOU'VE MADE IT! GREAT JOB!

I'm so very proud of you. Enjoy today because you've earned it. Tomorrow, we'll take these lessons and CREATE a bright future. Remember, this next year will bring challenges and opportunities. How you CHOOSE to handle them defines you. So, attack life. I encourage it.